Be Happy

Dona Herweck Rice

Publishing Credits

Rachelle Cracchiolo, M.S.Ed., *Publisher*
Conni Medina, M.A.Ed., *Managing Editor*
Nika Fabienke, Ed.D., *Content Director*
Véronique Bos, *Creative Director*
Shaun N. Bernadou, *Art Director*
Carol Huey-Gatewood, M.A.Ed., *Editor*
Valerie Morales, *Associate Editor*
Courtney Roberson, *Senior Graphic Designer*

Image Credits: All images from iStock and/or Shutterstock.

Teacher Created Materials
5301 Oceanus Drive
Huntington Beach, CA 92649-1030
www.tcmpub.com

ISBN 978-1-4938-9812-1

Printed in China 51497

Be  with a  .

happy slide

Be  with a .

happy swing

Be  with a  .

happy

book

Be  with a  .

happy

video game

Be  with a  .

happy ladybug

Be  with a  .

happy

butterfly

Be  with a  .

happy carrot

Be  with a  .

happy strawberry

Be  with a  .

happy cat

Be  with a .

happy

friend

High-Frequency Words

a

be

with